INVENTIONS AND DISCOVERY

THOMAS EDISON and the LIGHTBULB

by Scott R. Welvaert

illustrated by Phil Miller and
Charles Barnett III

Consultant:
Hal Wallace
Historian, Electricity Collections
National Museum of American History
Smithsonian Institution, Washington, D.C.

Capstone
press

Mankato, Minnesota

Graphic Library is published by Capstone Press,
1710 Roe Crest Drive, North Mankato, Minnesota 56003
www.capstonepub.com

Library of Congress Cataloging-in-Publication Data
Welvaert, Scott R.
   Thomas Edison and the lightbulb / by Scott Welvaert; illustrated by Phil Miller and
Charles Barnett III.
   p. cm.—(Graphic library. Inventions and discovery)
   Summary: "In graphic novel format, tells the story of Thomas Edison's involvement in
the development of the incandescent lightbulb"—Provided by publisher.
   Includes bibliographical references and index.
   ISBN-13: 978-0-7368-6489-3 (hardcover)
   ISBN-10: 0-7368-6489-X (hardcover)
   ISBN-13: 978-0-7368-9651-1 (softcover pbk.)
   ISBN-10: 0-7368-9651-1 (softcover pbk.)
   1. Edison, Thomas A. (Thomas Alva), 1847–1931—Juvenile literature. 2. Inventors—
United States—Biography—Juvenile literature. 3. Electric engineering—United States—
History—Juvenile literature. I. Title. II. Series.
TK140.E3P37 2007
621.3092—dc22

2006006976

Art Direction and Design
Bob Lentz

Colorist
Buzz Setzer

Editor
Christopher Harbo

Printed in the United States of America in Stevens Point, Wisconsin.
052013   007427R

TABLE OF CONTENTS

Chapter 1

The Quest for the Lightbulb

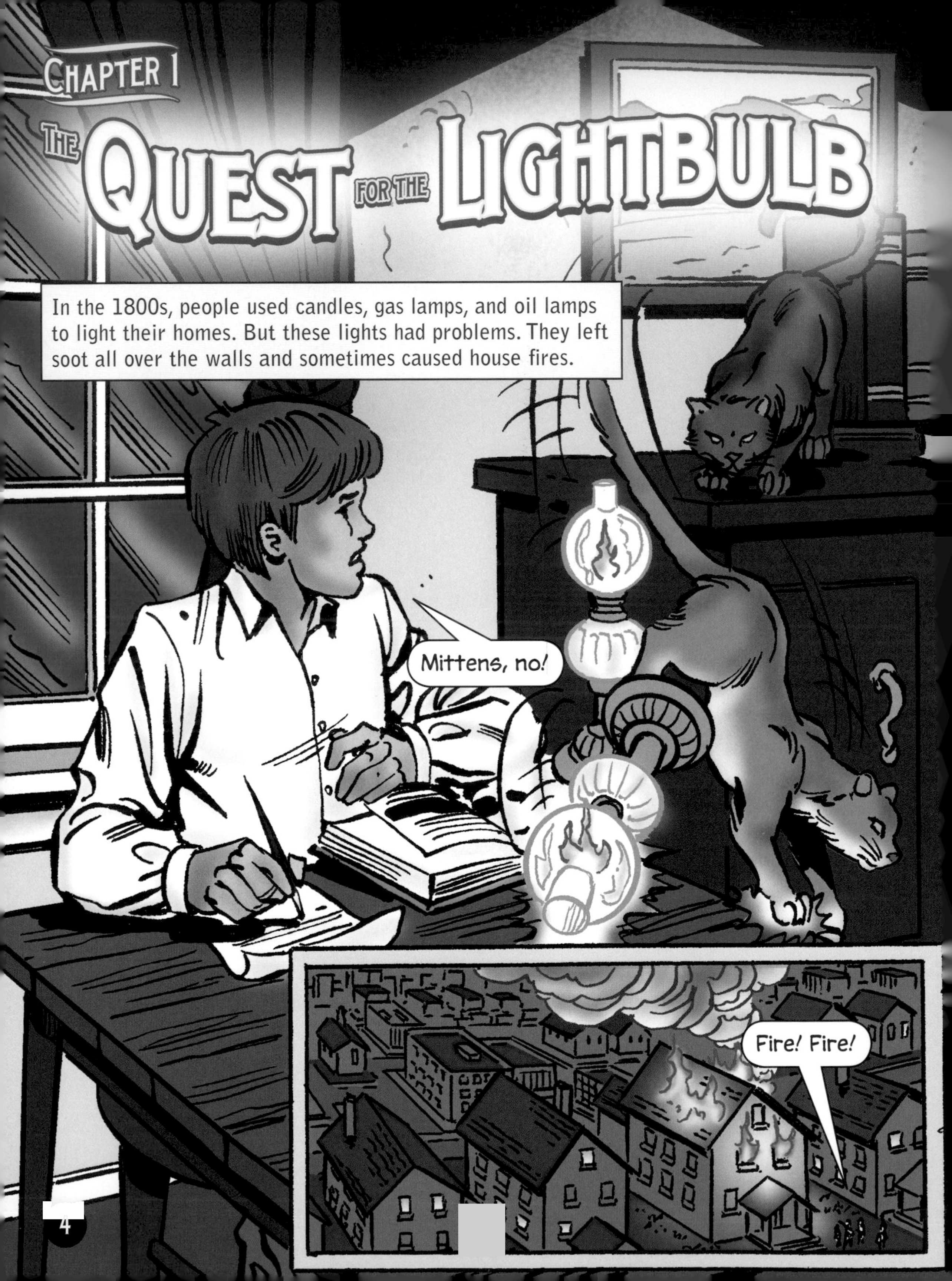

In the 1800s, people used candles, gas lamps, and oil lamps to light their homes. But these lights had problems. They left soot all over the walls and sometimes caused house fires.
Mittens, no!
Fire! Fire!

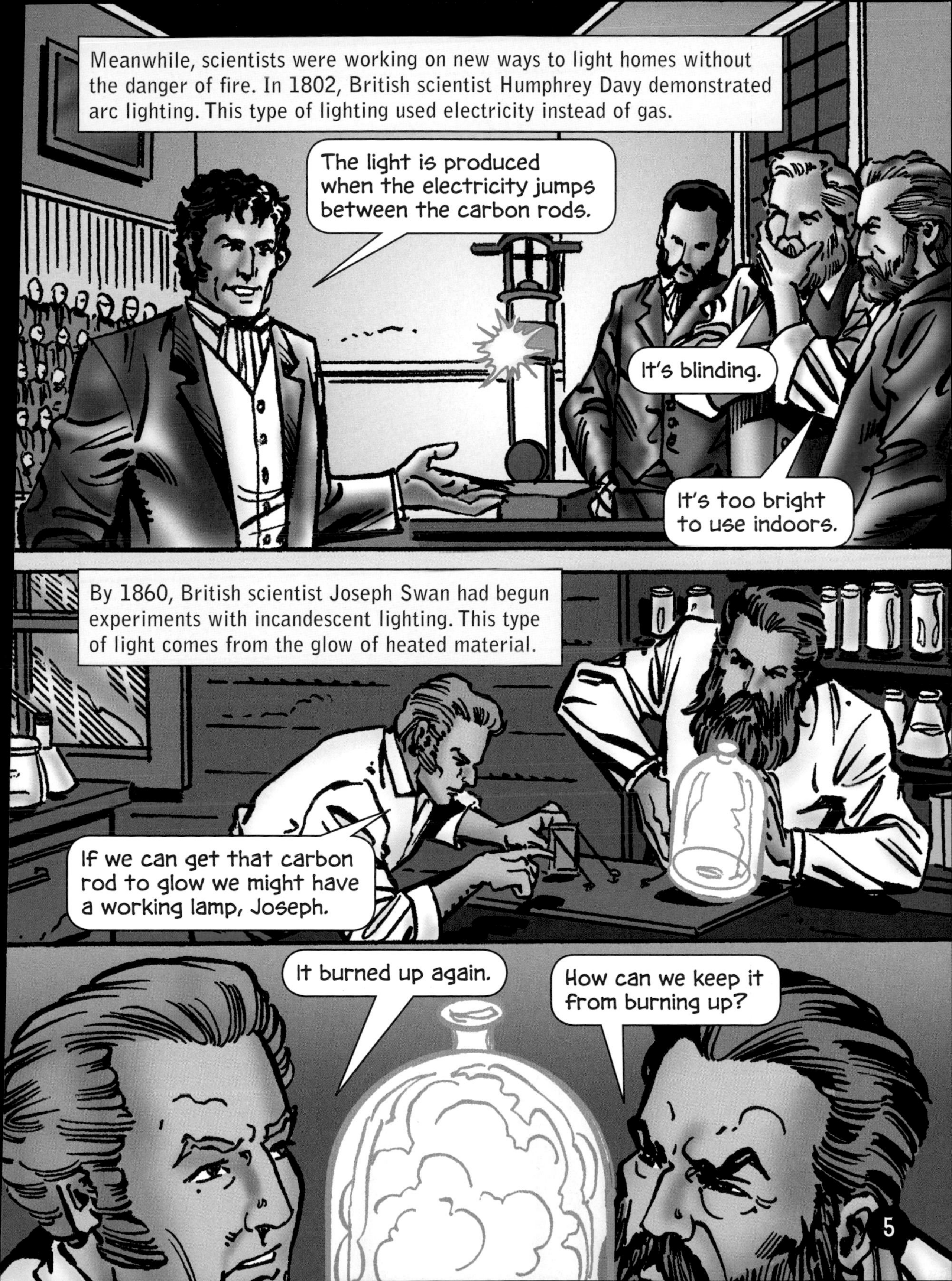
Meanwhile, scientists were working on new ways to light homes without the danger of fire. In 1802, British scientist Humphrey Davy demonstrated arc lighting. This type of lighting used electricity instead of gas.
The light is produced when the electricity jumps between the carbon rods.
It's blinding.
It's too bright to use indoors.
By 1860, British scientist Joseph Swan had begun experiments with incandescent lighting. This type of light comes from the glow of heated material.
If we can get that carbon rod to glow we might have a working lamp, Joseph.
It burned up again.
How can we keep it from burning up?

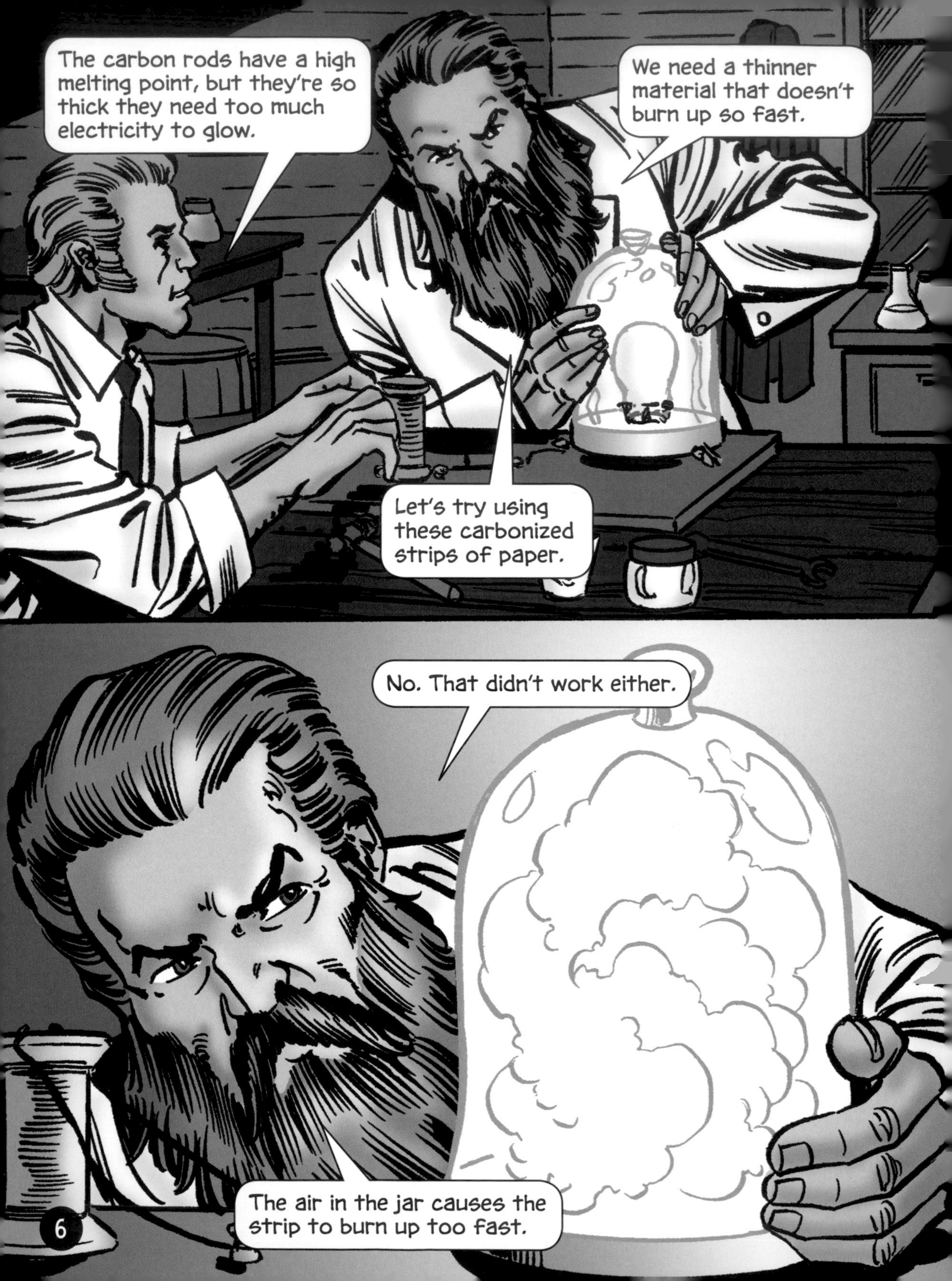
The carbon rods have a high melting point, but they're so thick they need too much electricity to glow.
We need a thinner material that doesn't burn up so fast.
Let's try using these carbonized strips of paper.
No. That didn't work either.
The air in the jar causes the strip to burn up too fast.

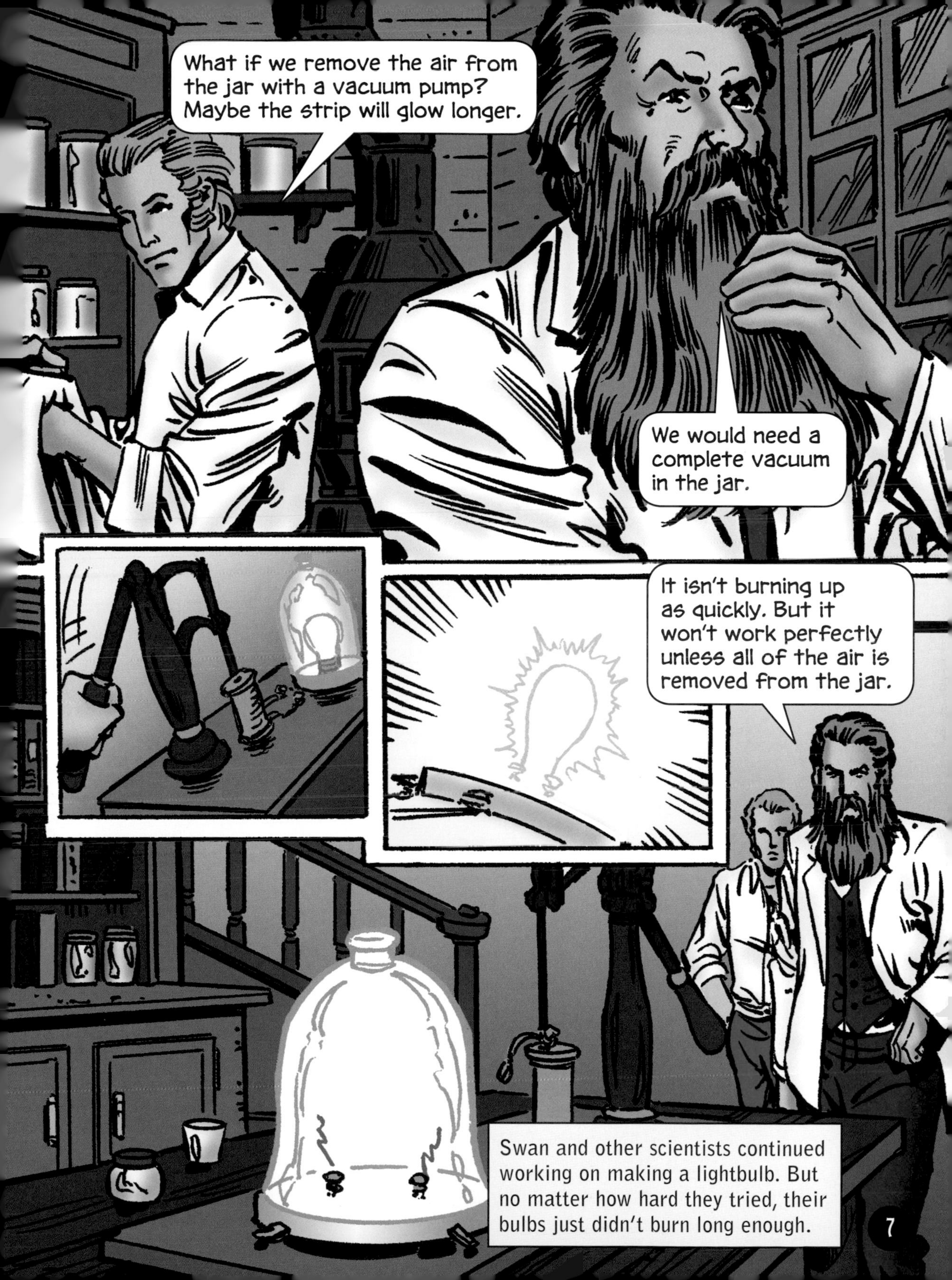
What if we remove the air from the jar with a vacuum pump? Maybe the strip will glow longer.
We would need a complete vacuum in the jar.
It isn't burning up as quickly. But it won't work perfectly unless all of the air is removed from the jar.
Swan and other scientists continued working on making a lightbulb. But no matter how hard they tried, their bulbs just didn't burn long enough.

Chapter 2
Edison Joins the Race

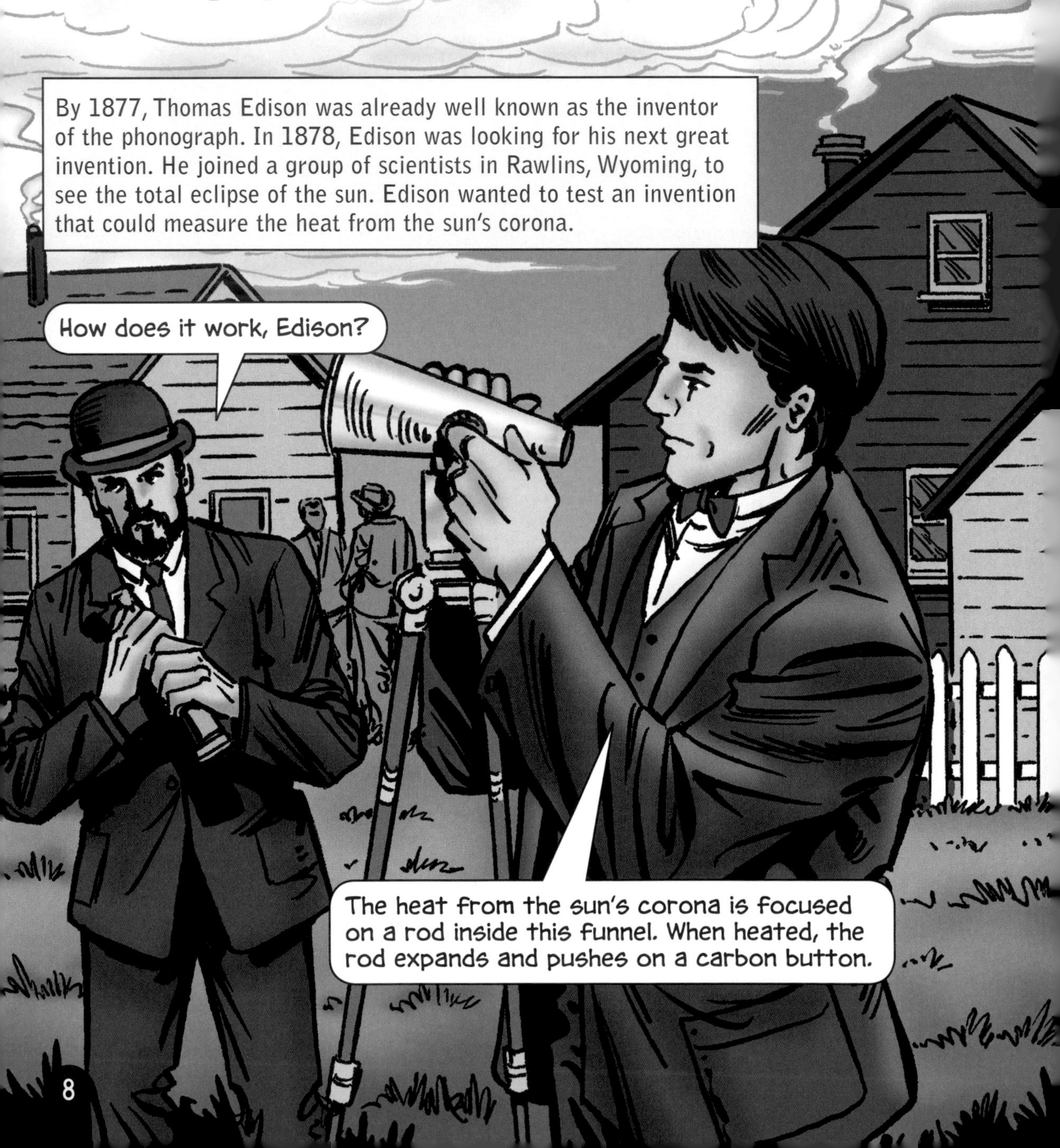
By 1877, Thomas Edison was already well known as the inventor of the phonograph. In 1878, Edison was looking for his next great invention. He joined a group of scientists in Rawlins, Wyoming, to see the total eclipse of the sun. Edison wanted to test an invention that could measure the heat from the sun's corona.
How does it work, Edison?
The heat from the sun's corona is focused on a rod inside this funnel. When heated, the rod expands and pushes on a carbon button.

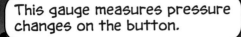

This gauge measures pressure changes on the button.

I can calculate the heat from the corona based on the gauge's readings.

Amazing!

With another success under his belt, Edison relaxed with his fellow scientists.

You know, Thomas, I've heard some scientists are close to perfecting an electric lamp. Just imagine a city lit up like these stars light up the sky.

It would be beautiful. But building a lamp is only half the problem. You would need a reliable supply of electrical power as well.

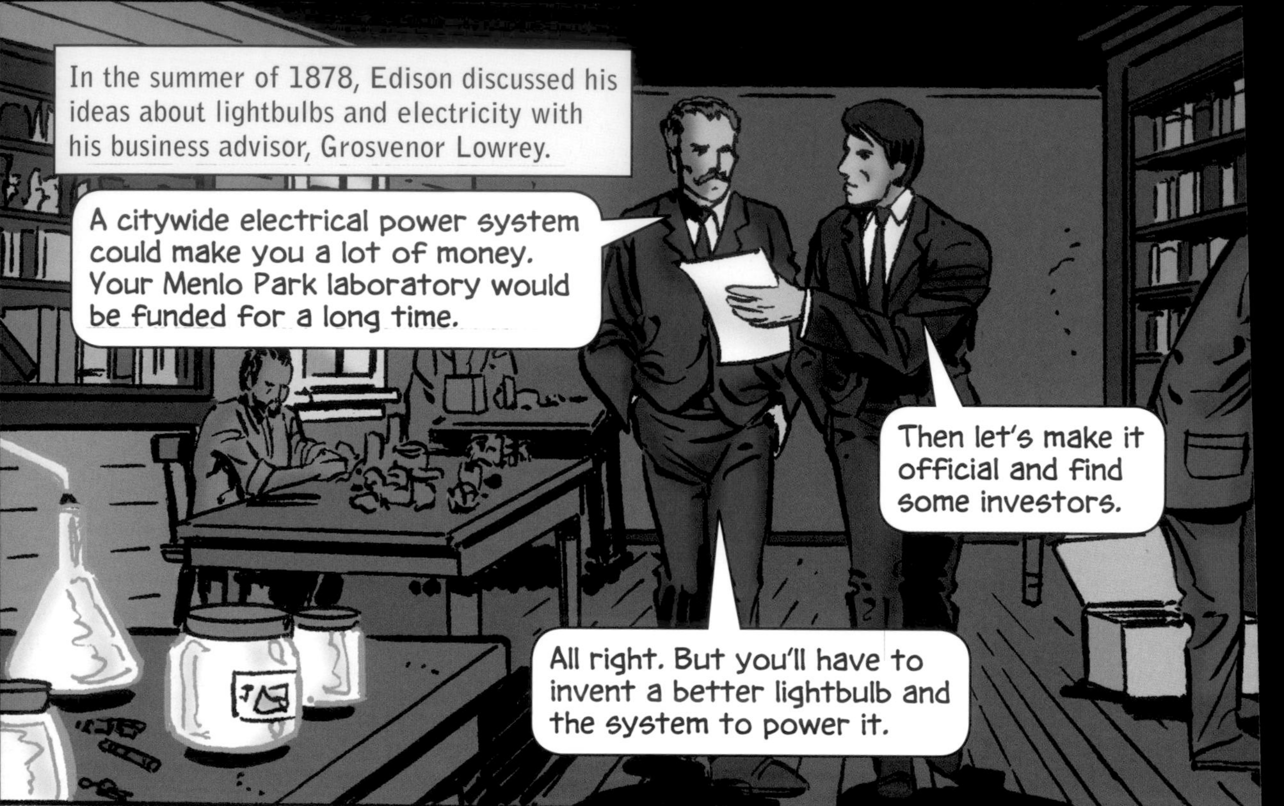
In the summer of 1878, Edison discussed his ideas about lightbulbs and electricity with his business advisor, Grosvenor Lowrey.
A citywide electrical power system could make you a lot of money. Your Menlo Park laboratory would be funded for a long time.
Then let's make it official and find some investors.
All right. But you'll have to invent a better lightbulb and the system to power it.

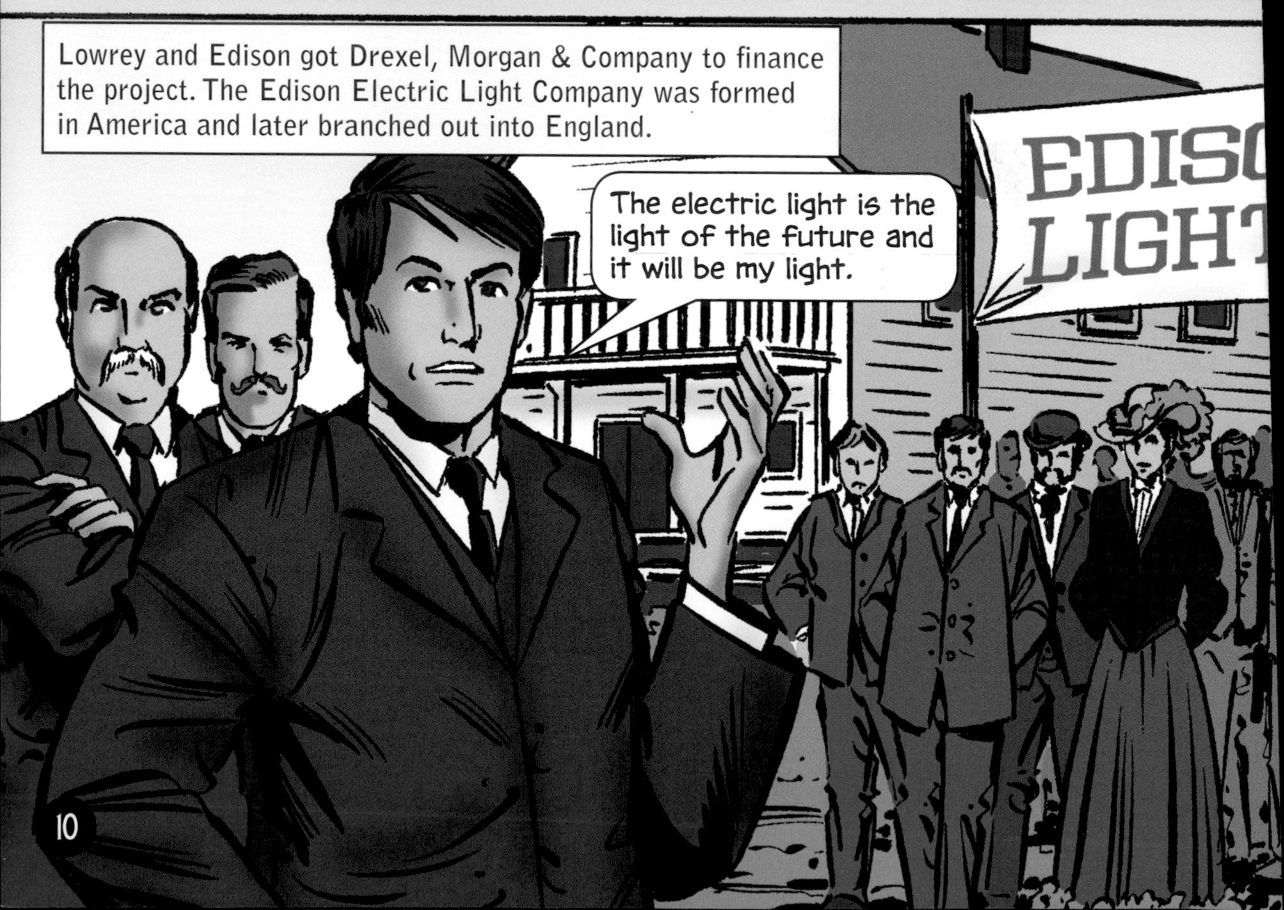
Lowrey and Edison got Drexel, Morgan & Company to finance the project. The Edison Electric Light Company was formed in America and later branched out into England.
The electric light is the light of the future and it will be my light.

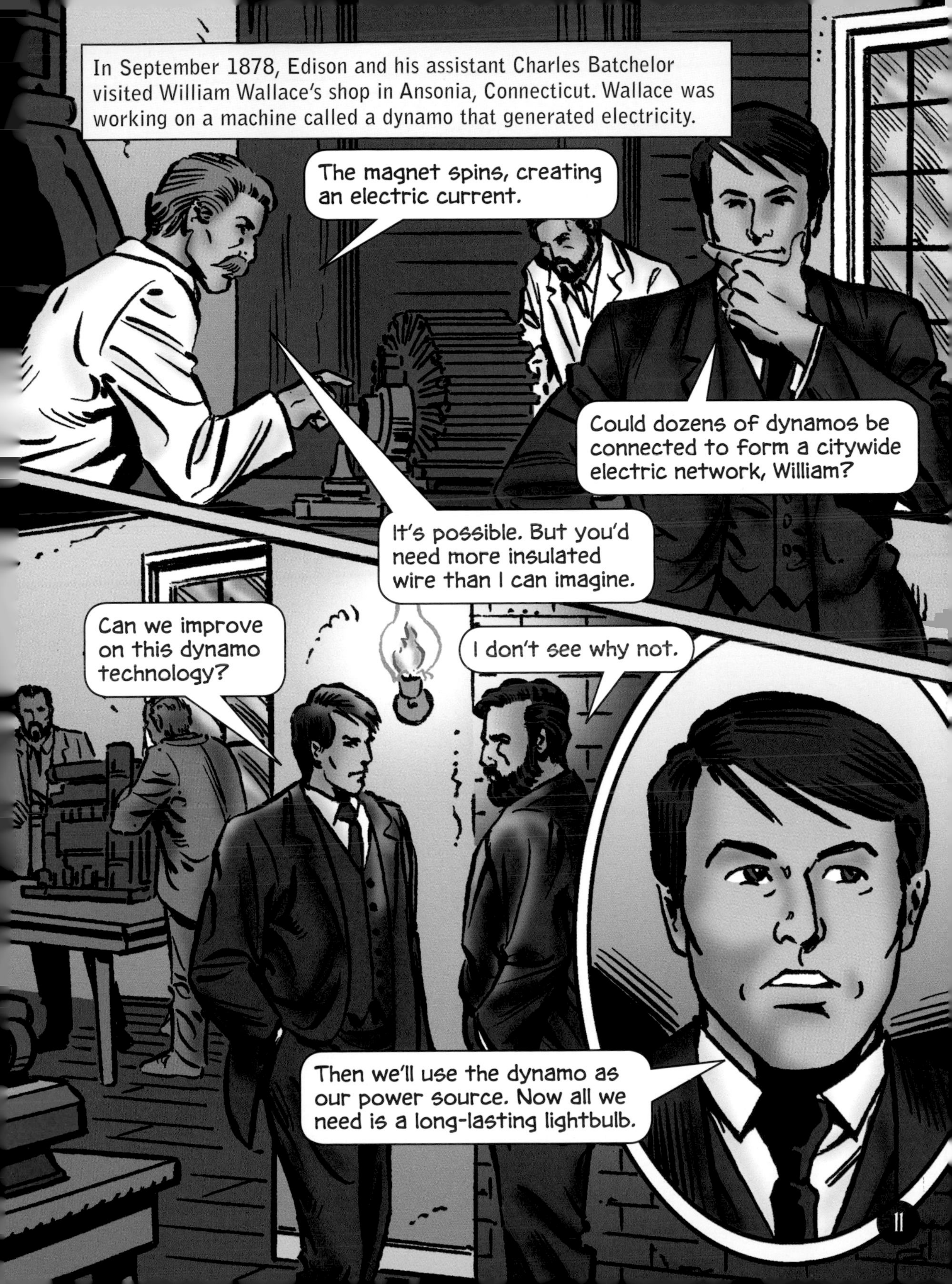
In September 1878, Edison and his assistant Charles Batchelor visited William Wallace's shop in Ansonia, Connecticut. Wallace was working on a machine called a dynamo that generated electricity.
The magnet spins, creating an electric current.
Could dozens of dynamos be connected to form a citywide electric network, William?
It's possible. But you'd need more insulated wire than I can imagine.
Can we improve on this dynamo technology?
I don't see why not.
Then we'll use the dynamo as our power source. Now all we need is a long-lasting lightbulb.

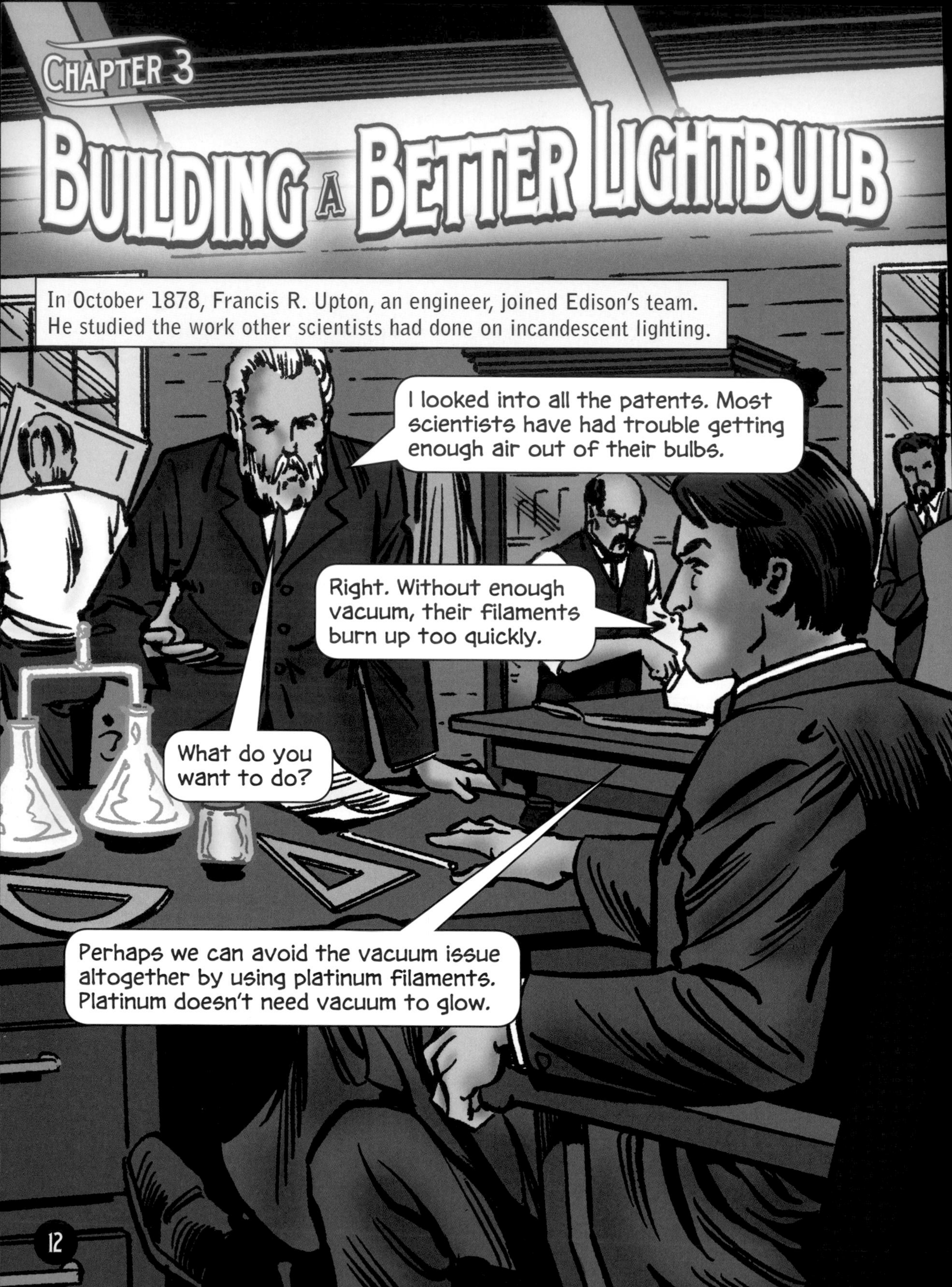
CHAPTER 3
BUILDING A BETTER LIGHTBULB
In October 1878, Francis R. Upton, an engineer, joined Edison's team. He studied the work other scientists had done on incandescent lighting.
I looked into all the patents. Most scientists have had trouble getting enough air out of their bulbs.
Right. Without enough vacuum, their filaments burn up too quickly.
What do you want to do?
Perhaps we can avoid the vacuum issue altogether by using platinum filaments. Platinum doesn't need vacuum to glow.

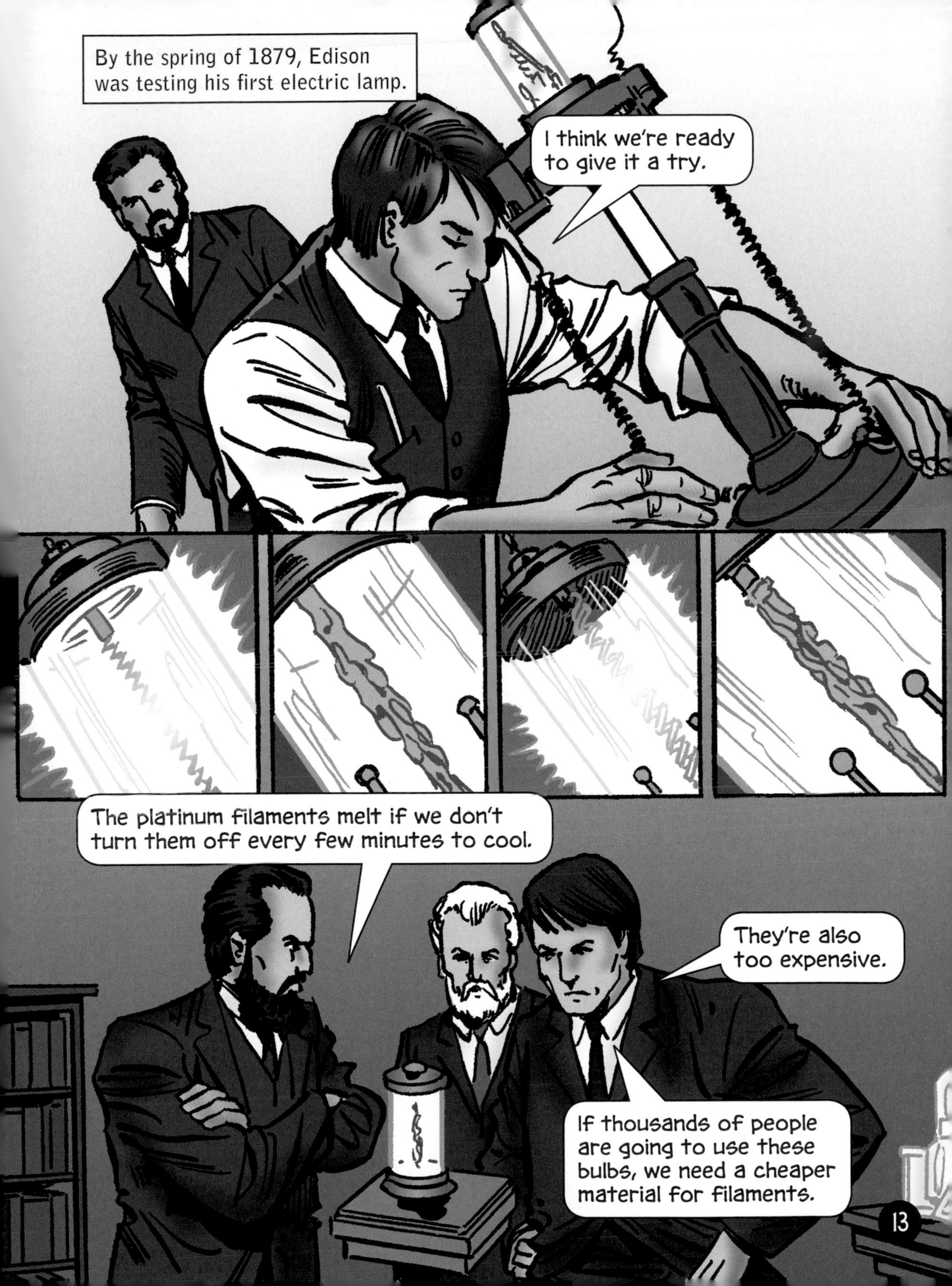
By the spring of 1879, Edison was testing his first electric lamp.
I think we're ready to give it a try.
The platinum filaments melt if we don't turn them off every few minutes to cool.
They're also too expensive.
If thousands of people are going to use these bulbs, we need a cheaper material for filaments.

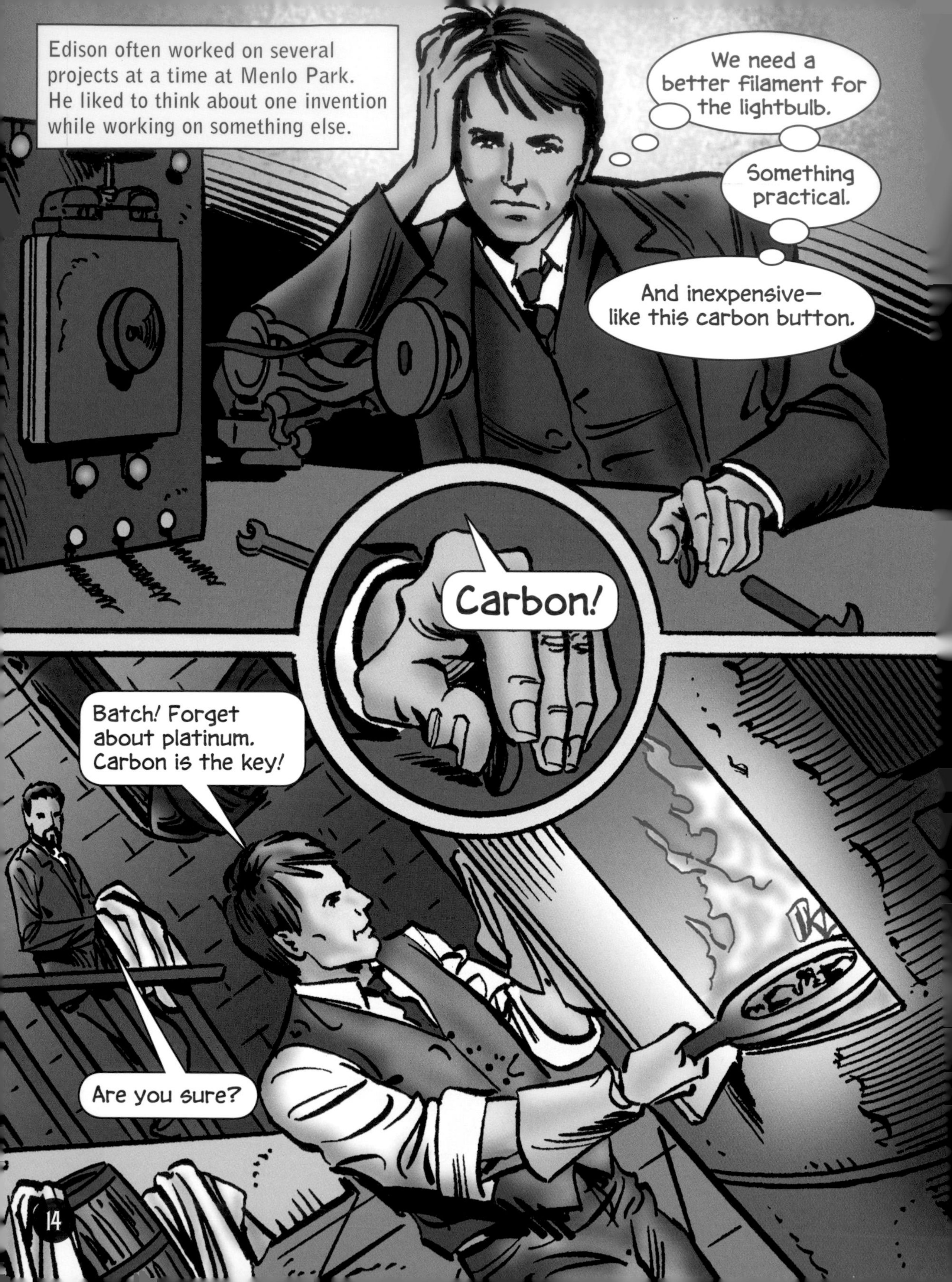
Edison often worked on several projects at a time at Menlo Park. He liked to think about one invention while working on something else.
We need a better filament for the lightbulb.
Something practical.
And inexpensive—like this carbon button.
Carbon!
Batch! Forget about platinum. Carbon is the key!
Are you sure?

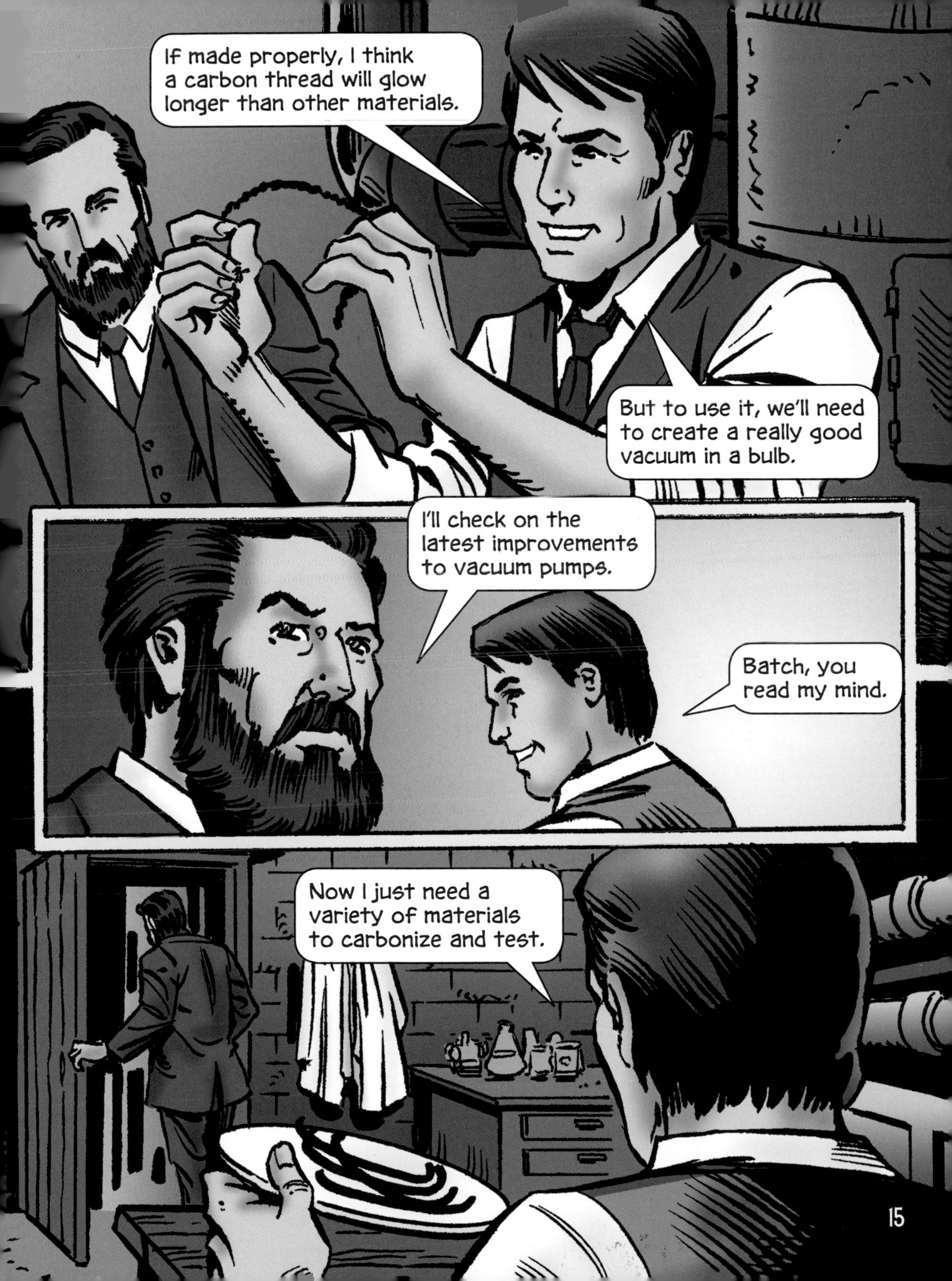

If made properly, I think a carbon thread will glow longer than other materials.
But to use it, we'll need to create a really good vacuum in a bulb.
I'll check on the latest improvements to vacuum pumps.
Batch, you read my mind.
Now I just need a variety of materials to carbonize and test.

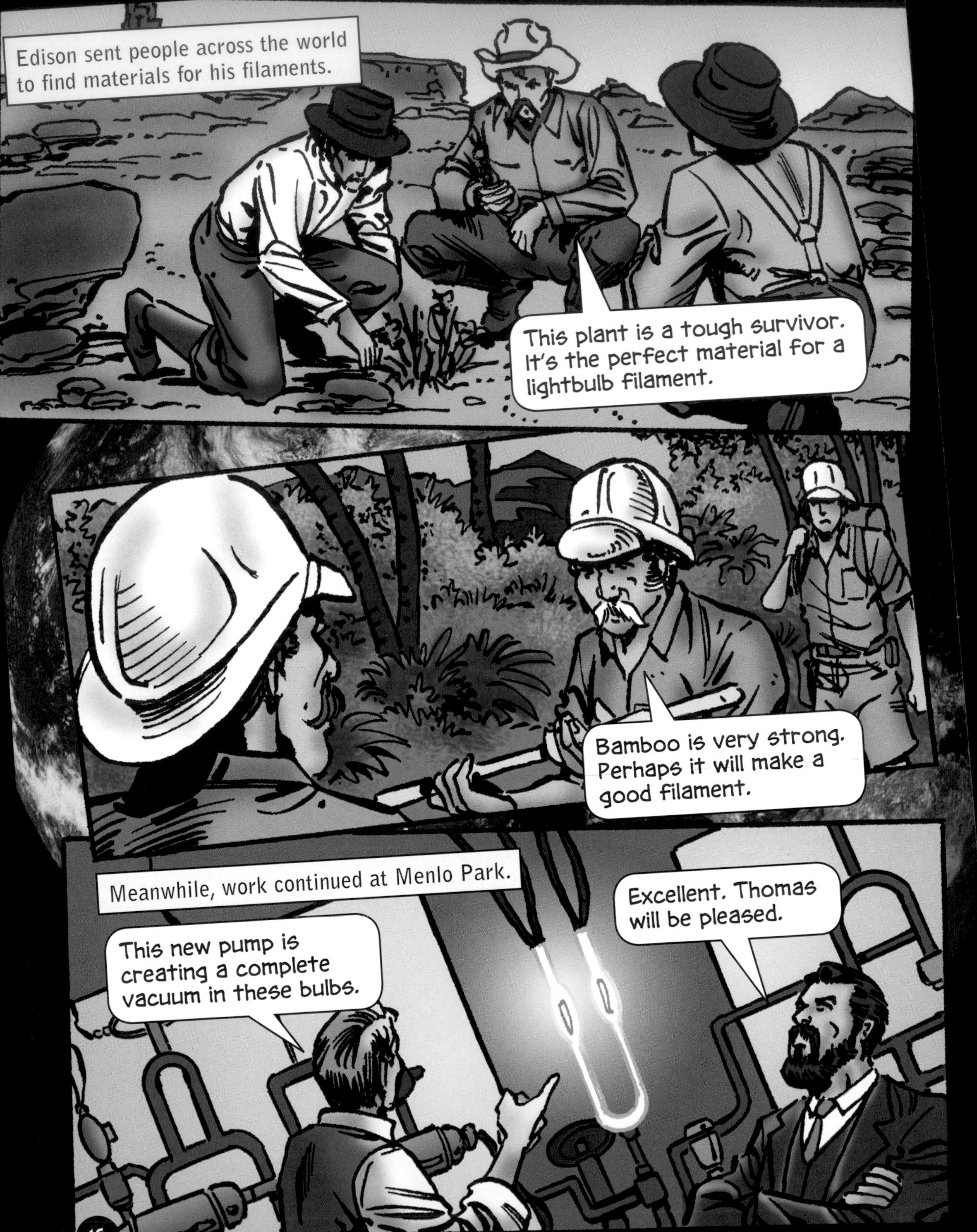
Edison sent people across the world to find materials for his filaments.
This plant is a tough survivor. It's the perfect material for a lightbulb filament.
Bamboo is very strong. Perhaps it will make a good filament.
Meanwhile, work continued at Menlo Park.
This new pump is creating a complete vacuum in these bulbs.
Excellent. Thomas will be pleased.

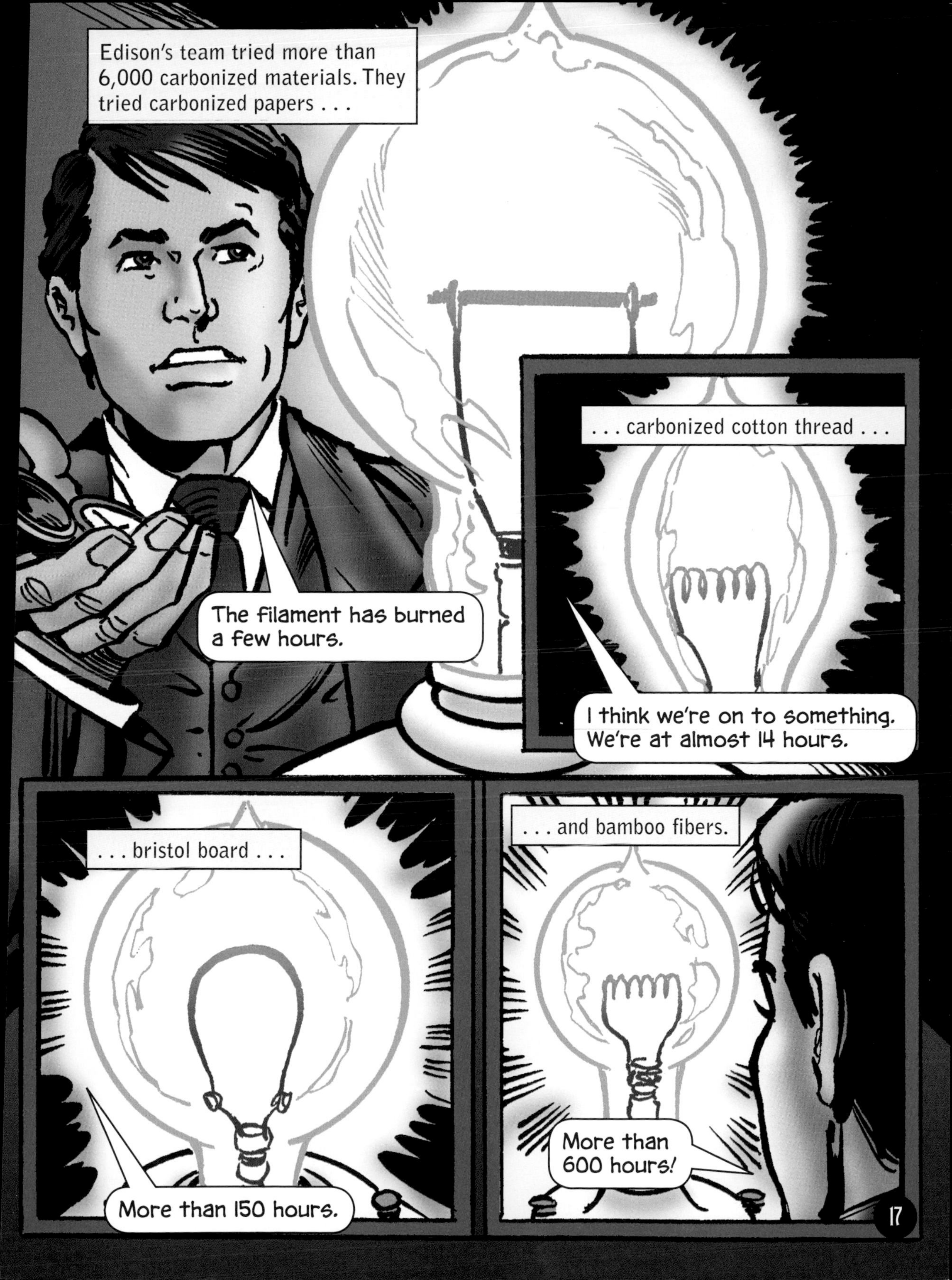
Edison's team tried more than 6,000 carbonized materials. They tried carbonized papers . . .
The filament has burned a few hours.
. . . carbonized cotton thread . . .
I think we're on to something. We're at almost 14 hours.
. . . bristol board . . .
More than 150 hours.
. . . and bamboo fibers.
More than 600 hours!

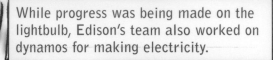

While progress was being made on the lightbulb, Edison's team also worked on dynamos for making electricity.

How are things coming with the dynamo?

Our tests are going well. It's making enough electricity to light hundreds of lightbulbs.

Excellent!

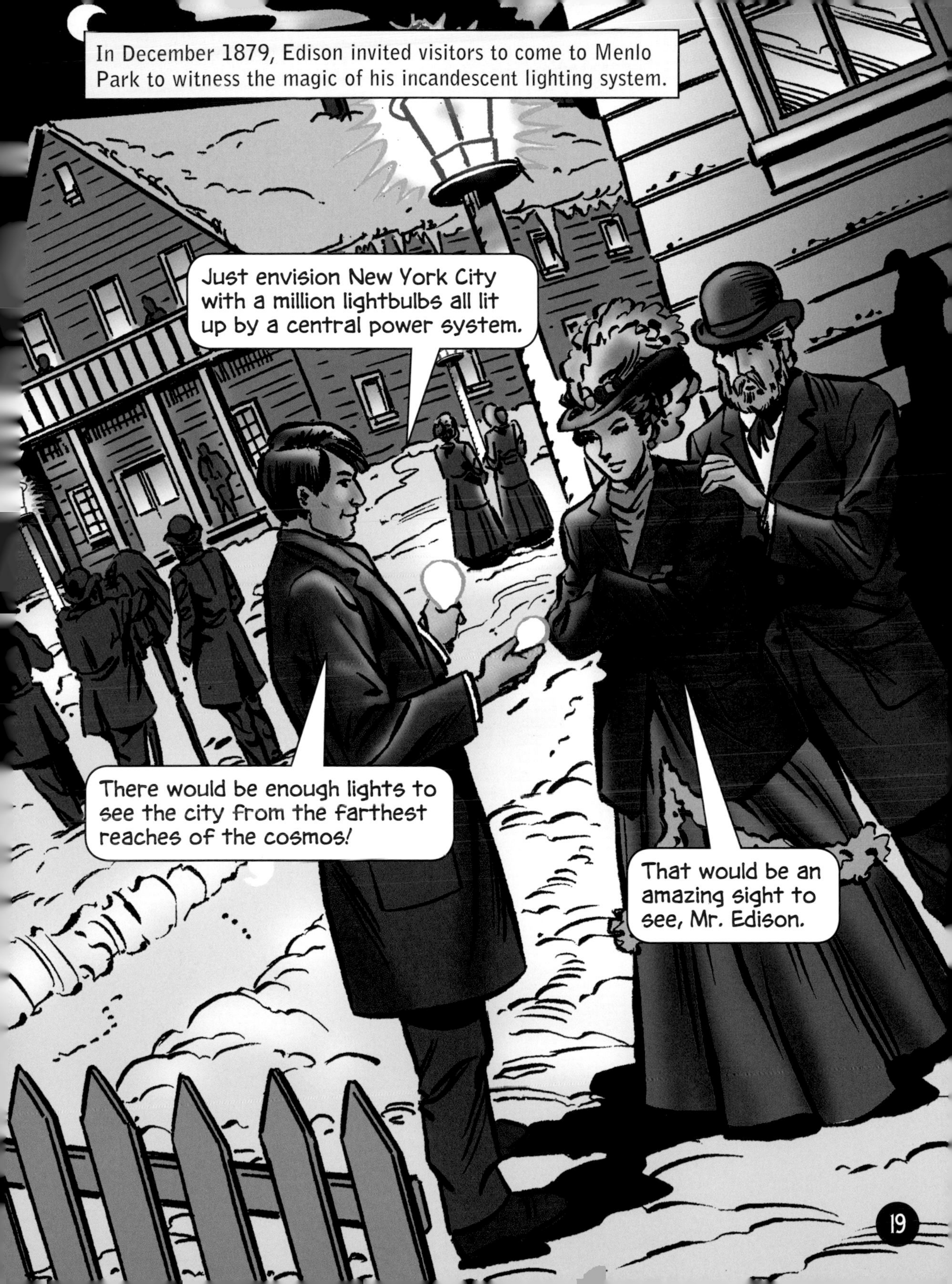
In December 1879, Edison invited visitors to come to Menlo Park to witness the magic of his incandescent lighting system.
Just envision New York City with a million lightbulbs all lit up by a central power system.
There would be enough lights to see the city from the farthest reaches of the cosmos!
That would be an amazing sight to see, Mr. Edison.

Chapter 4
Lighting the World

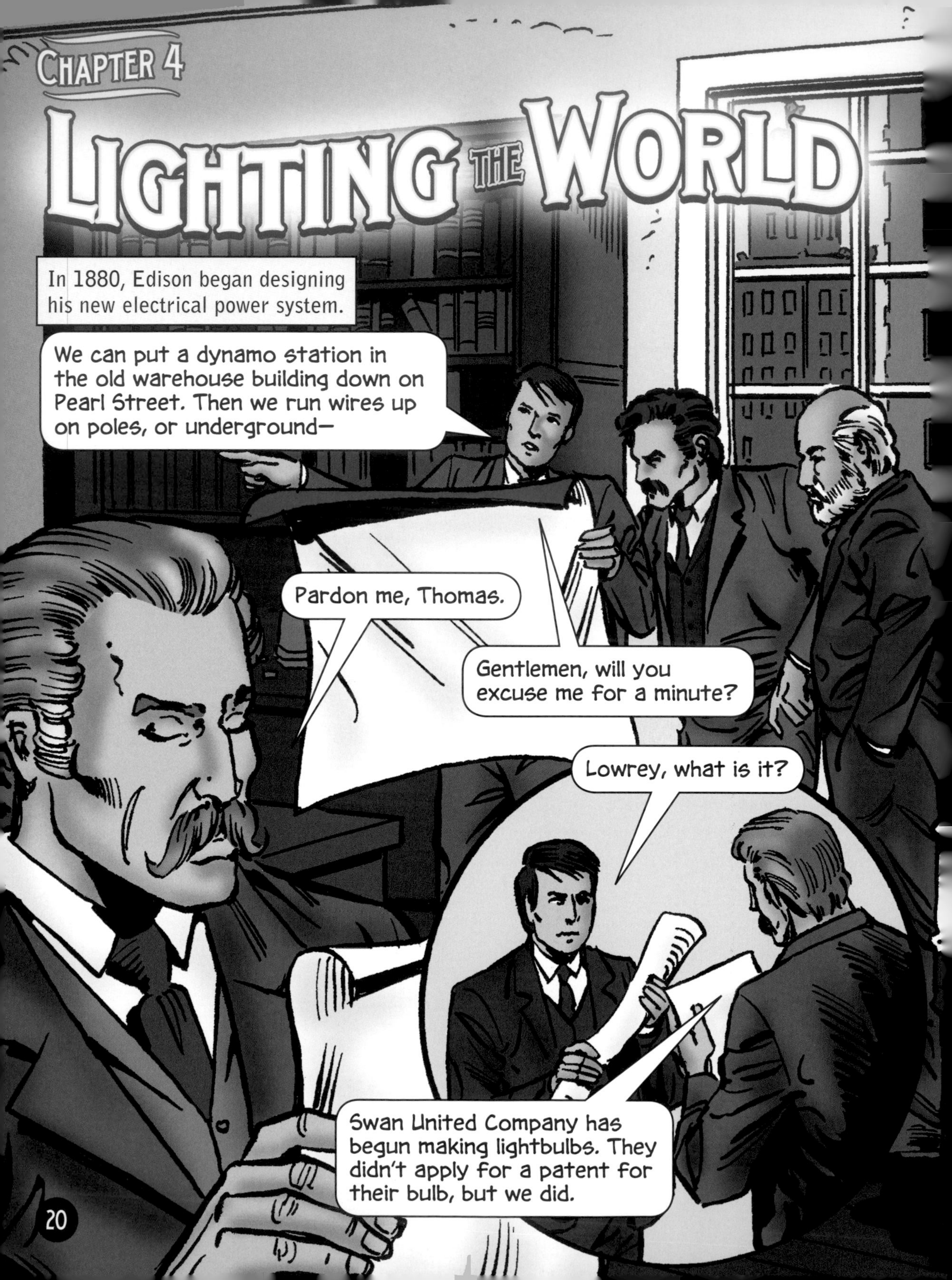
In 1880, Edison began designing his new electrical power system.
We can put a dynamo station in the old warehouse building down on Pearl Street. Then we run wires up on poles, or underground—
Pardon me, Thomas.
Gentlemen, will you excuse me for a minute?
Lowrey, what is it?
Swan United Company has begun making lightbulbs. They didn't apply for a patent for their bulb, but we did.

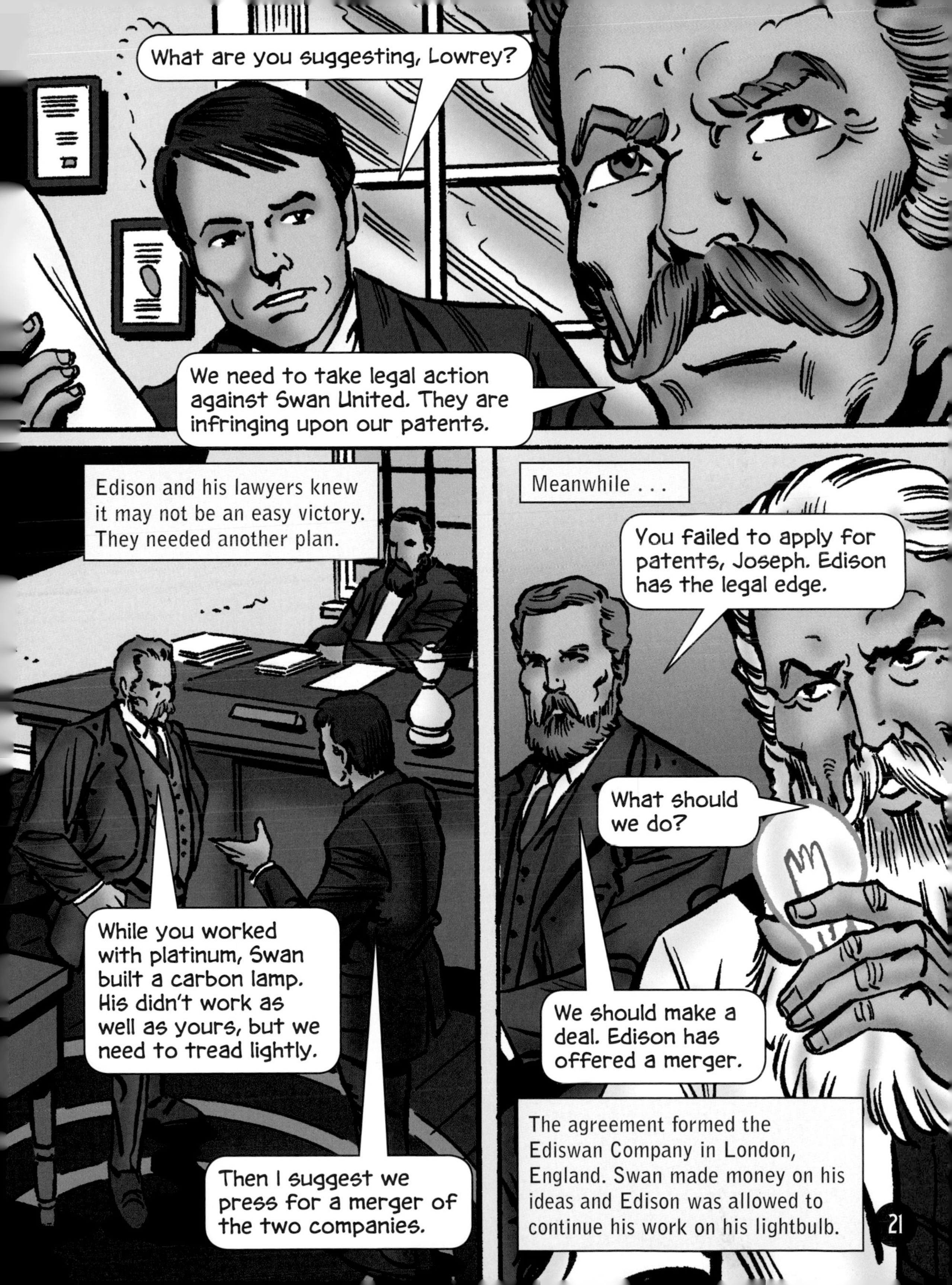

What are you suggesting, Lowrey?
We need to take legal action against Swan United. They are infringing upon our patents.
Edison and his lawyers knew it may not be an easy victory. They needed another plan.
While you worked with platinum, Swan built a carbon lamp. His didn't work as well as yours, but we need to tread lightly.
Then I suggest we press for a merger of the two companies.
Meanwhile . . .
You failed to apply for patents, Joseph. Edison has the legal edge.
What should we do?
We should make a deal. Edison has offered a merger.
The agreement formed the Ediswan Company in London, England. Swan made money on his ideas and Edison was allowed to continue his work on his lightbulb.

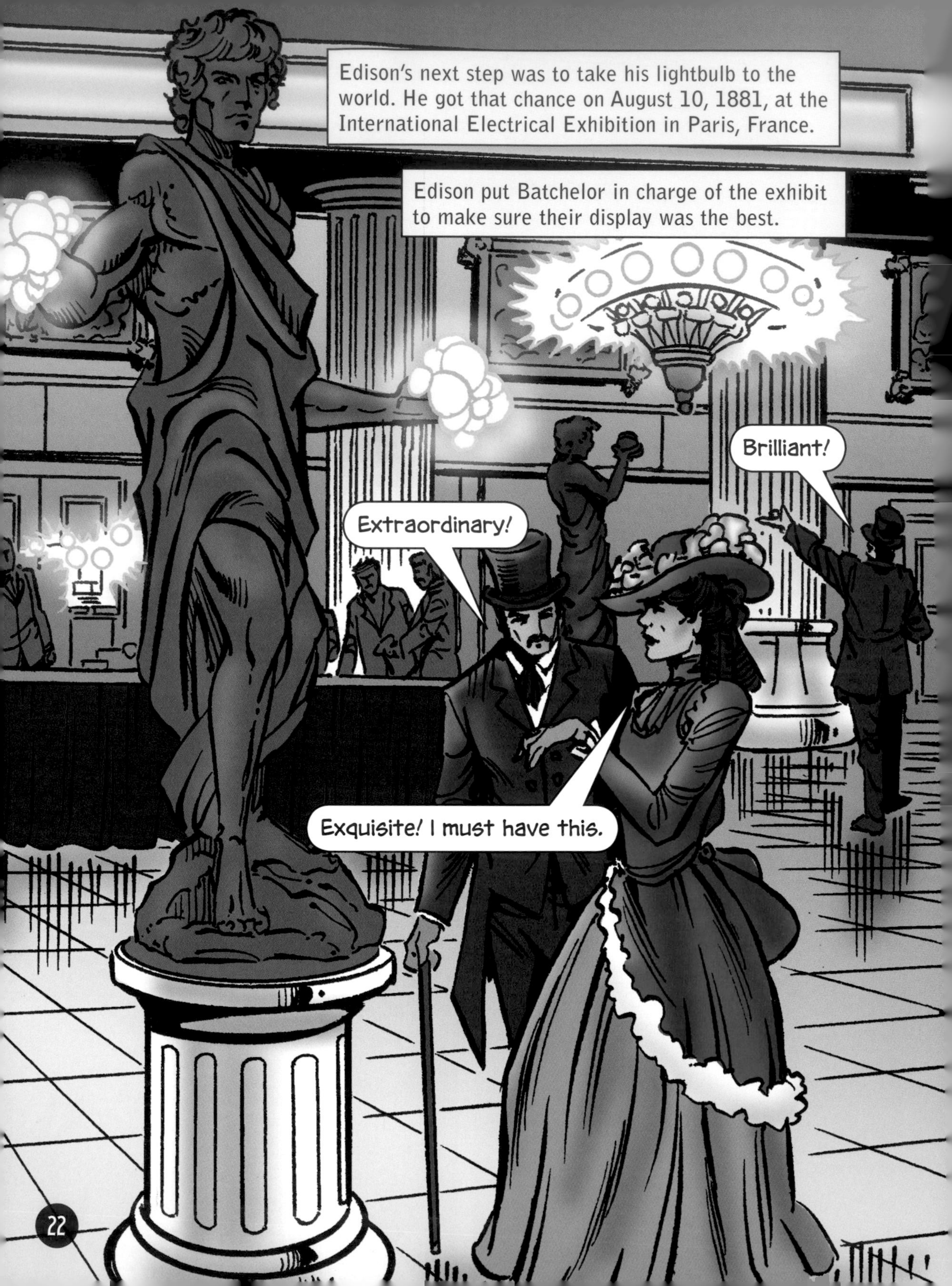
Edison's next step was to take his lightbulb to the world. He got that chance on August 10, 1881, at the International Electrical Exhibition in Paris, France.
Edison put Batchelor in charge of the exhibit to make sure their display was the best.
Brilliant!
Extraordinary!
Exquisite! I must have this.

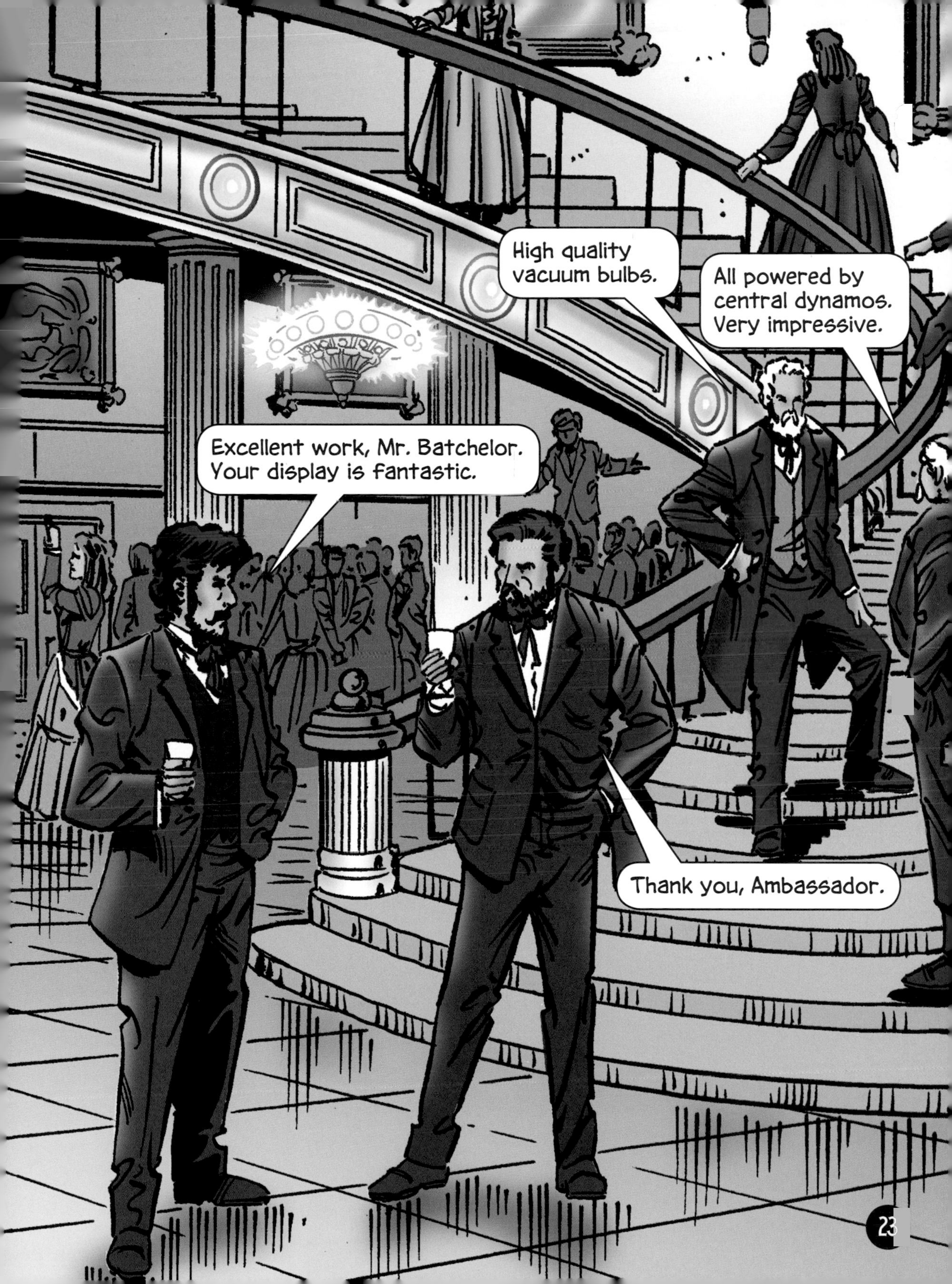
High quality vacuum bulbs.
All powered by central dynamos. Very impressive.
Excellent work, Mr. Batchelor. Your display is fantastic.
Thank you, Ambassador.

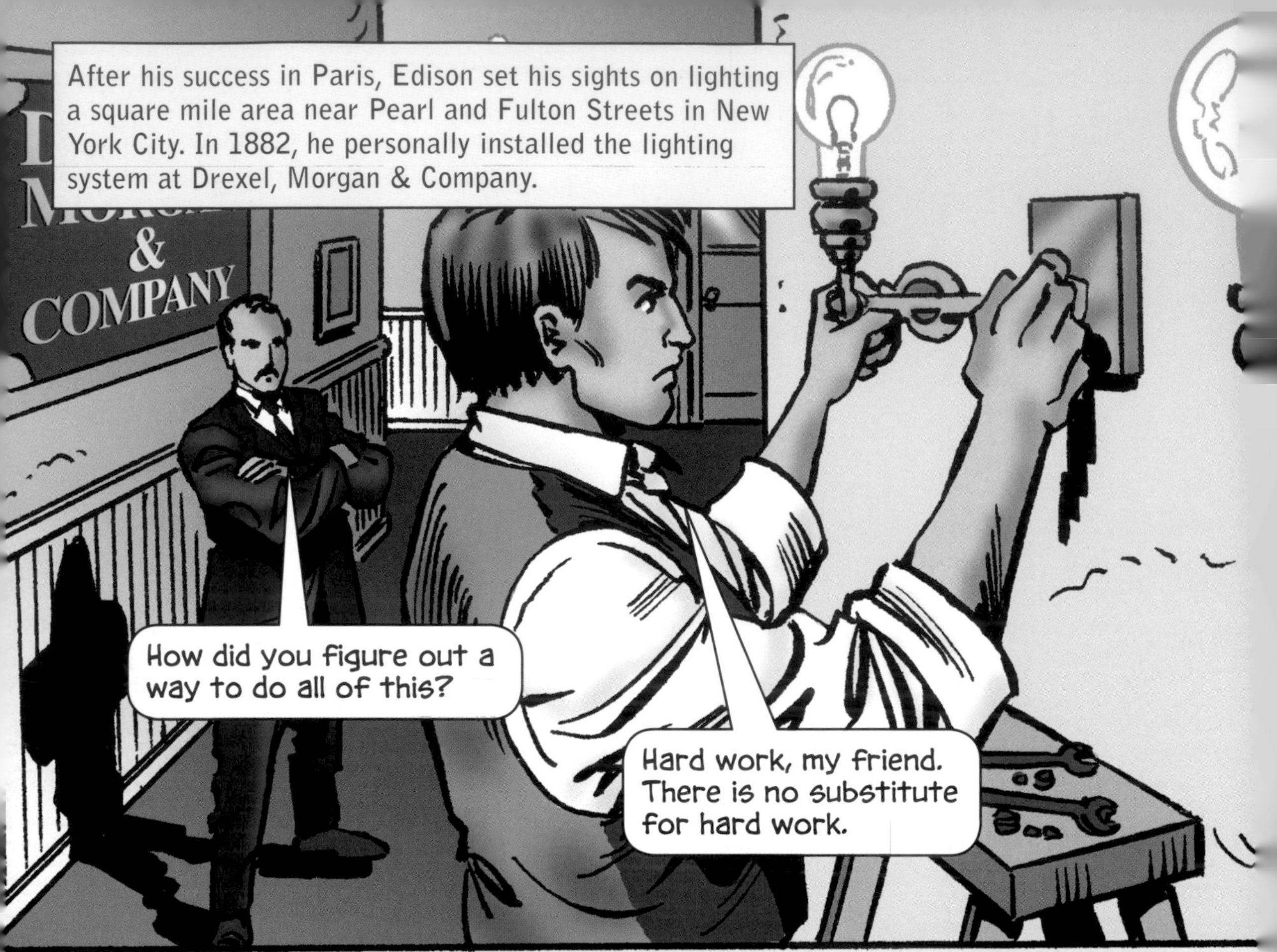
After his success in Paris, Edison set his sights on lighting a square mile area near Pearl and Fulton Streets in New York City. In 1882, he personally installed the lighting system at Drexel, Morgan & Company.
& COMPANY
How did you figure out a way to do all of this?
Hard work, my friend. There is no substitute for hard work.

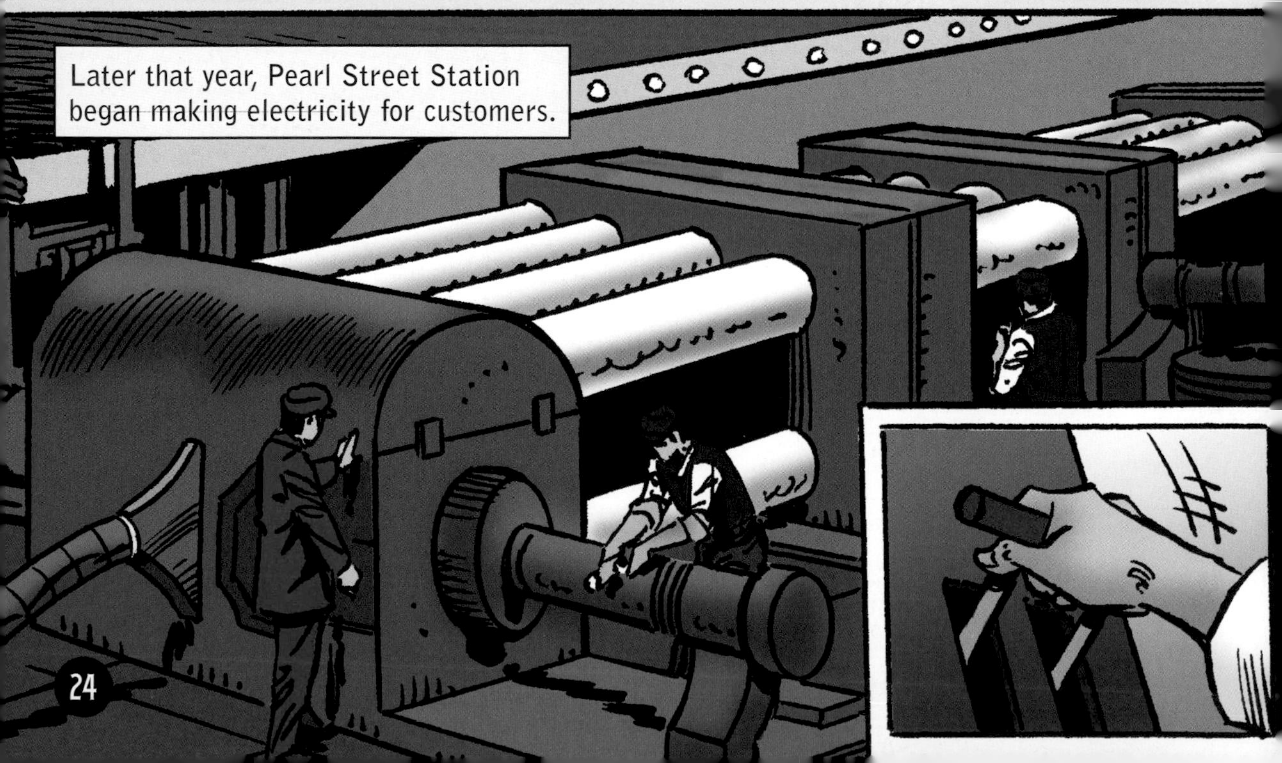
Later that year, Pearl Street Station began making electricity for customers.

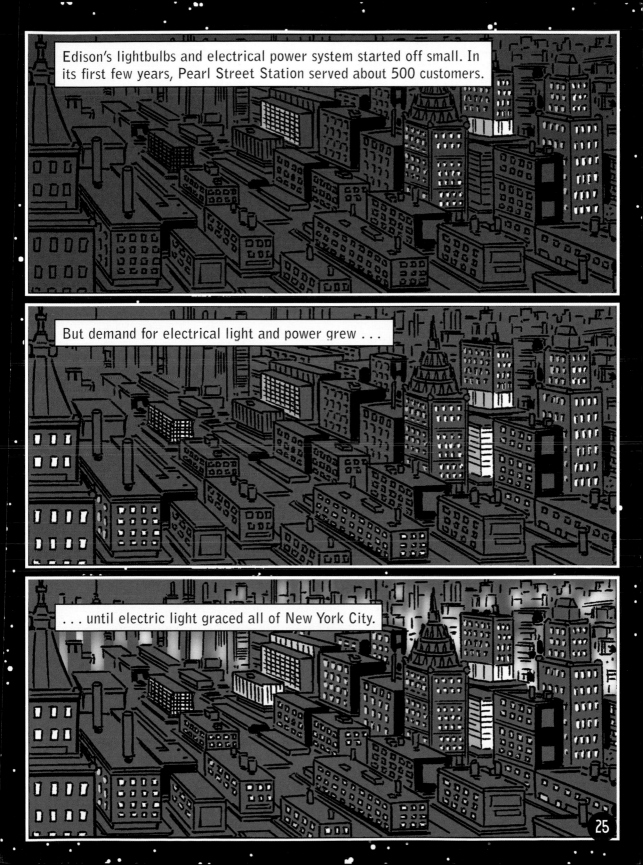

Edison's lightbulbs and electrical power system started off small. In its first few years, Pearl Street Station served about 500 customers.

But demand for electrical light and power grew . . .

. . . until electric light graced all of New York City.

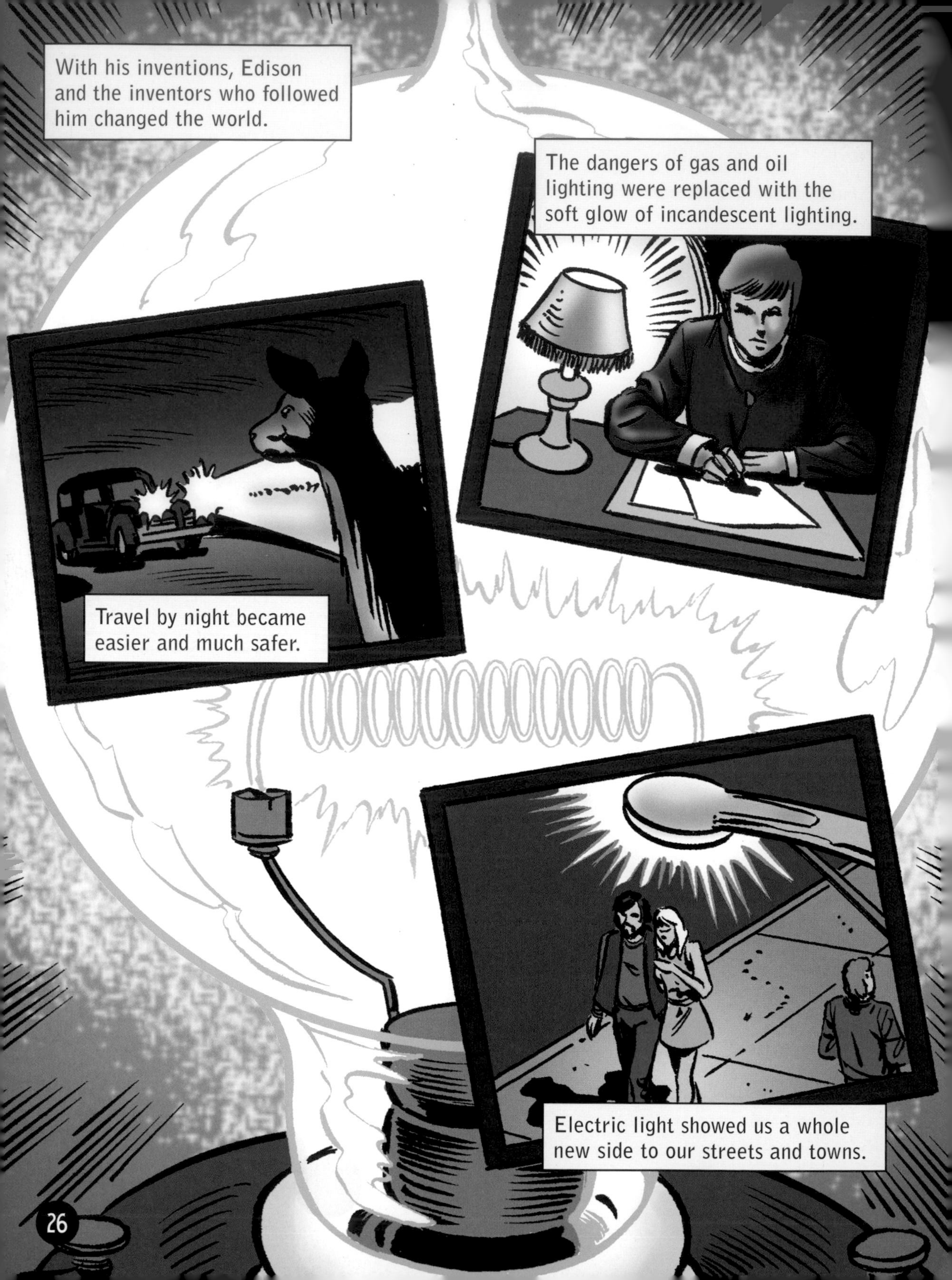
With his inventions, Edison and the inventors who followed him changed the world.
The dangers of gas and oil lighting were replaced with the soft glow of incandescent lighting.
Travel by night became easier and much safer.
Electric light showed us a whole new side to our streets and towns.

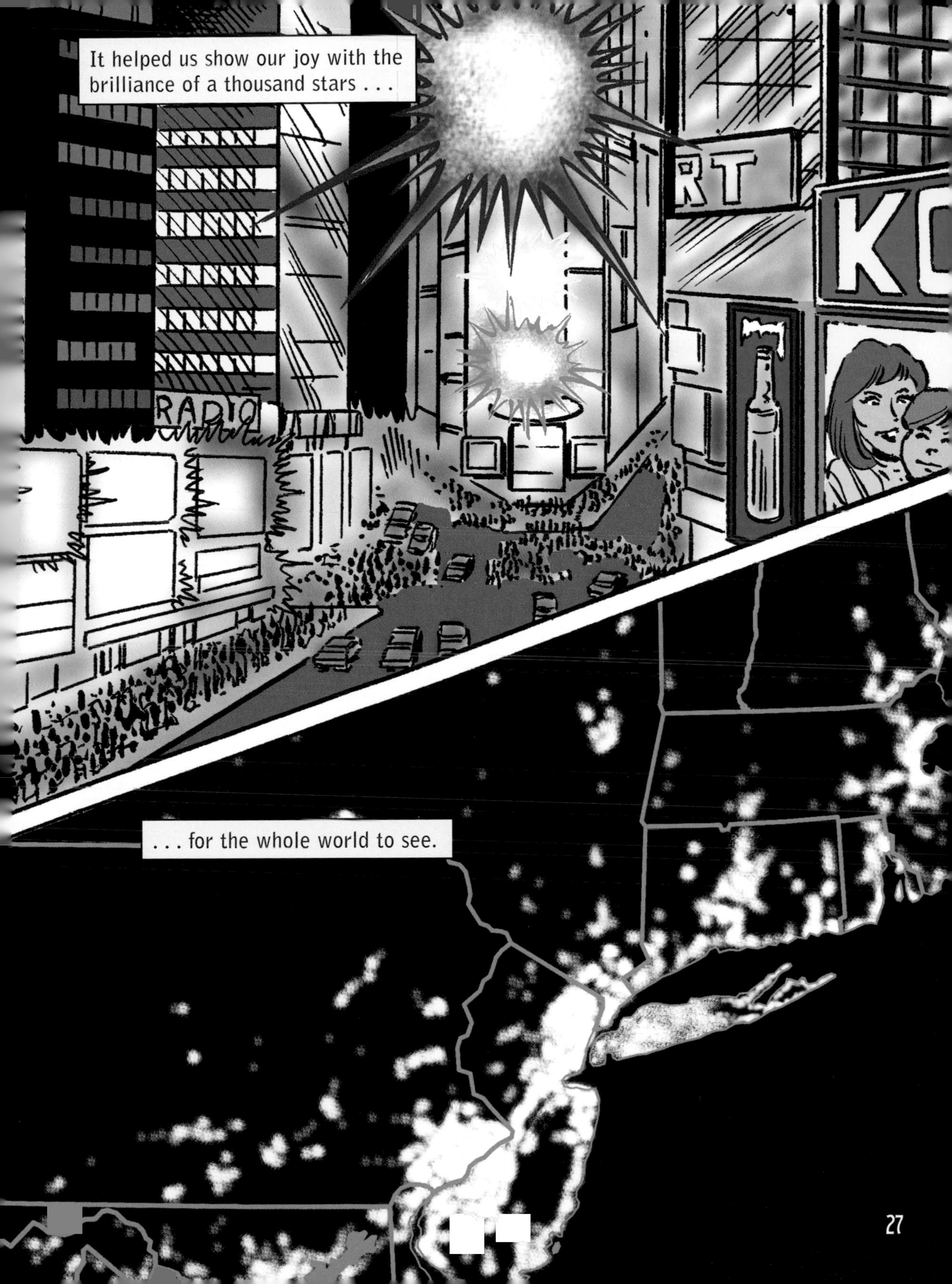
It helped us show our joy with the brilliance of a thousand stars . . .
RADIO
. . . for the whole world to see.

MORE ABOUT THOMAS EDISON and the LIGHTBULB

Thomas Alva Edison was born February 11, 1847, in Milan, Ohio. He died on October 18, 1931, in West Orange, New Jersey.

Edison opened his laboratory in Menlo Park, New Jersey, in 1876. His laboratory became known as the "invention factory" because Edison's staff often worked on more than one invention at a time. Because of his amazing inventions, newspapers called Edison the "Wizard of Menlo Park."

Edison patented 1,093 inventions in his lifetime. Besides the lightbulb, he developed the phonograph for recording and playing sounds. He also invented the movie camera and made some of the world's first silent movies.

Edison's first lightbulbs burned for less than 100 hours. Eventually, he produced a lightbulb that burned for more than 1,500 hours.

The lightbulb was only one part of Edison's effort to bring electric light to the world. He also developed circuit breakers, transmission lines, fuses, light sockets, and light switches to make electric light safe and easy to use.

- Edison developed a dynamo he called Jumbo to create electricity in his Pearl Street Station. The Jumbo dynamo was four times as large as any dynamo built at the time. It produced enough electricity to power 1,200 lights. Pearl Street Station used six Jumbo dynamos to supply power to 1 square mile (2.6 square kilometers) of New York City.

- Near his laboratory, Edison had factories that made some of his inventions. In 1882, Edison's factories made about 100,000 lightbulbs. But demand for electric light grew quickly. In 1900, his factories made 45 million lightbulbs.

- When Pearl Street Station opened in 1882, it served 85 customers with about 400 lightbulbs. Fourteen months later, the power station served 508 customers with more than 12,700 lightbulbs.

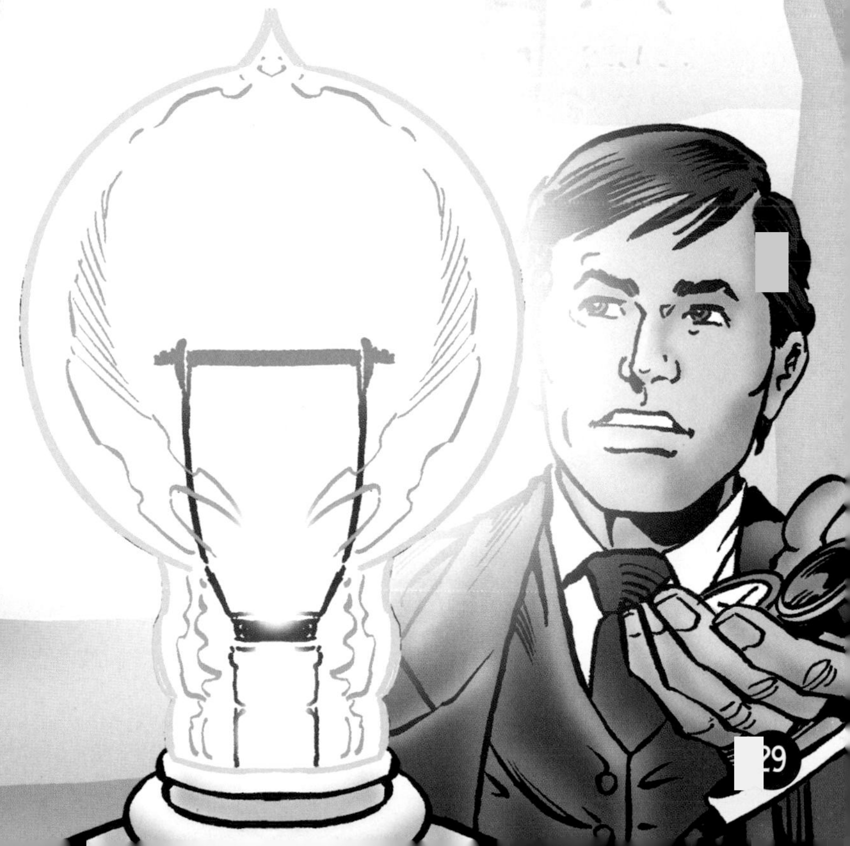

GLOSSARY

carbon (KAR-buhn)—an element found in diamonds, coal, and living plants and animals; carbon filaments were made by baking materials until they turned into pure carbon.

corona (kuh-ROH-nuh)—the outermost part of the sun's atmosphere

dynamo (DYE-nuh-moh)—a machine for converting the power of a turning wheel into electricity

filament (FIL-uh-muhnt)—a thin wire that is heated electrically to produce light

incandescent (in-kan-DESS-uhnt)—glowing with strong light and heat

patent (PAT-ent)—a document that protects people's inventions so others cannot steal the ideas

vacuum (VAK-yoom)—a sealed space emptied of air or gas

INTERNET SITES

FactHound offers a safe, fun way to find Internet sites related to this book. All of the sites on FactHound have been researched by our staff.

Here's how:
1. Visit *www.facthound.com*
2. Choose your grade level.
3. Type in this book ID **073686489X** for age-appropriate sites. You may also browse subjects by clicking on letters, or by clicking on pictures and words.
4. Click on the **Fetch It** button.

FactHound will fetch the best sites for you!

READ MORE

Cefrey, Holly. *The Inventions of Thomas Alva Edison: Father of the Light Bulb and the Motion Picture Camera.* Reading Power. New York: PowerKids Press, 2003.

Nobleman, Marc Tyler. *The Light Bulb.* Great Inventions. Mankato, Minn.: Capstone Press, 2004.

Price-Groff, Claire. *Thomas Alva Edison: Inventor and Entrepreneur.* Great Life Stories. New York: Franklin Watts, 2003.

Raatma, Lucia. *Thomas Edison.* Early Biographies. Minneapolis: Compass Point Books, 2004.

BIBLIOGRAPHY

Baldwin, Neil. *Edison: Inventing the Century.* Chicago: University of Chicago Press, 2001.

Friedel, Robert, and Paul Israel. *Edison's Electric Light: Biography of an Invention.* New Brunswick, N.J.: Rutgers University Press, 1986.

Josephson, Matthew. *Edison: A Biography.* New York: McGraw-Hill, 1959.

Millard, A. J. *Edison and the Business of Innovation.* Baltimore: Johns Hopkins University Press, 1990.

INDEX